The SHIPBUILDERS

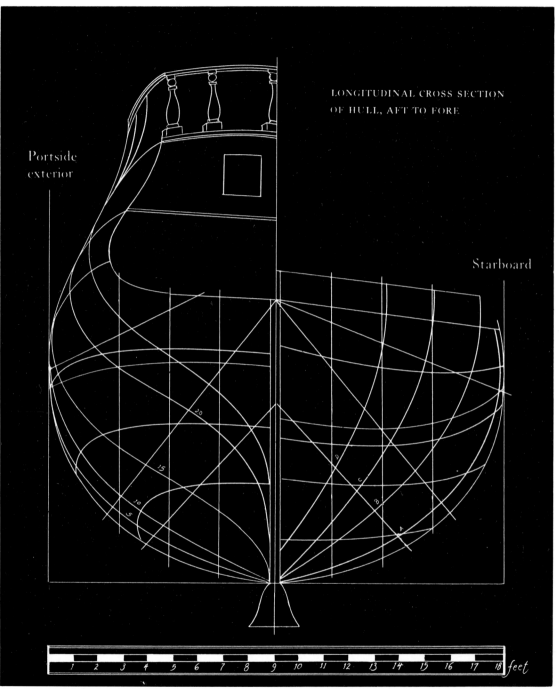

Portside
exterior

LONGITUDINAL CROSS SECTION
OF HULL, AFT TO FORE

Starboard

20

15

10

5

1 2 3 4 5 6 7 8 9 10 11 12 13 14 15 16 17 18 *feet*

A typical eighteenth-century draft of a small vessel,
showing cross-sectional design from the after end of the ship.
The vessel's beam (greatest width) is shown as 18 feet.

COLONIAL CRAFTSMEN

The
SHIPBUILDERS

WRITTEN & ILLUSTRATED BY

Leonard Everett Fisher

BENCHMARK BOOKS

MARSHALL CAVENDISH
NEW YORK

Benchmark Books
Marshall Cavendish Corporation
99 White Plains Road
Tarrytown, New York 10591

Copyright © 1971 by Leonard Everett Fisher

First Marshall Cavendish edition 1998

Library of Congress Cataloging-in-Publication Data
Fisher, Leonard Everett.
The shipbuilders / written & illustrated by Leonard Everett Fisher.
p.   cm. — (Colonial craftsmen)
Originally published: New York : F. Watts, 1971
Includes index.
Summary: Traces the history of shipbuilding in the American colonies and
describes each step in the building of an eighteenth-century ship.
ISBN 0-7614-0508-9
1. Shipbuilding—United States—History—Juvenile literature. [1. Shipbuilding—
History. 2. United States—History—Colonial period, ca. 1600–1775.]
I. Title. II. Series: Fisher, Leonard Everett. Colonial craftsmen.
VM23.F53   1998   623.8'2'097409033—dc20   96-36136   CIP   AC

Printed and bound in the United States of America

1   3   5   6   4   2

A Short History

It was August, 1607 — three months after the founding of Jamestown, Virginia, the first permanent English settlement in North America. Two British ships, *Gift of God* and *Mary and John*, were anchored off a rocky spit of land at the mouth of the Kennebec River in what is now Maine. This point and the river that ran through it were called Sagadahoc by the Indians who lived in the region.

The one hundred and twenty men on the two ships had been sent to the wild, rocky coast of northern New England by the Plymouth Company of London. They hoped to establish Britain's second permanent colony in North America. George Popham and Raleigh Gilbert led the adventurers. They had stopped briefly at the St. George's Islands, then had gone on to Sagadahoc. There they chose a site near present-day Popham Beach and immediately began to build their settlement.

By October, two months after their arrival, Fort St. George loomed above the rocks and tidal sands of Sagadahoc. Twelve cannons threatened whatever enemies lurked in the wilderness or rode the slapping waters of the river. Behind the palisaded walls of the fort were a church, a storehouse, and about a dozen dwelling houses.

Outside the walls, at the river's edge, stood the framework of a sleek *pinnace* — a small, lightweight coastal vessel. Some weeks later, the thirty-ton pinnace was completed. The Sagadahoc colonists named her *Virginia*. She was the first sailing ship to be built by the British in North America.

The *Virginia* was not designed for rough deepwater voyages. Yet she was so strongly constructed that she weathered a passage from Maine to England to carry a load of furs and sassafras root. On her return she began a career of discovery and trade along the North American coast.

The Sagadahoc colonists had made a seaworthy vessel out of the raw timber from the forest that crowded in on their tiny settlement. But the builders did not fare as well as their ship. Suffering from the biting winter weather, more than half the settlers deserted the colony. Those who remained were so discouraged that they left Sagadahoc in the fall of 1608 and returned to England with their ship, *Virginia*.

In 1614, the Dutch on Manhattan Island, now New York City, launched the first completely decked-over ship to be built in America — Captain Adriaen Block's *Onrust*.

Six years later, in 1620, a few British shipwrights arrived in Jamestown, Virginia. They hoped to put together some deepwater vessels and start a successful shipbuilding business. They managed to construct one or two *shallops* — something like oversized rowboats fitted with a sail — but they did not do much more. Whatever long voyages the early Virginians undertook were made in either Dutch or English ships.

The Pilgrims had arrived at Plymouth in the *Mayflower* in 1620. They succeeded in establishing Britain's second permanent colony in North America. Once the *Mayflower* had returned to England, the settlers felt the need of boats of their own. Their livelihood depended on fishing and fur trading, and for both they needed vessels that would take them along the coast. There was unlimited timber in the forests, and in 1624 a ship carpenter arrived in the colony. He set out to build several shallops and two *ketches* — small, two-masted boats. He was a good workman, but after he had built two strong shallops he died of fever.

The Pilgrims felt his loss greatly. They desperately needed a larger ship. In 1626, one of their regular carpenters sawed one of the shallops in two across the middle and put in planks to lengthen the boat five or six feet. He strengthened her with timbers, built her up, and laid a deck on her. She was fitted with sails and served the Pilgrims well for seven years.

The colonists of Salem, Massachusetts, were better equipped for shipbuilding. In 1629 they gave land and other favors to six master ship carpenters if they would settle there. Salem became an early center for shipbuilding.

In 1631, Puritan shipwrights at Medford, a town about fifty miles north of Plymouth, succeeded in building a thirty-ton armed merchant vessel. They called her *Blessing of the Bay*. With the launching of *Blessing of the Bay*, a true shipbuilding industry began in North America.

During the next ten years, small privately owned shipyards began to dot the New England coastline between the thick forests and the ocean. The many coves and inlets were perfect places for shipyards. And the forests reaching almost to the water's edge had stout oaks for ships' hulls, and tall, straight white pines for their masts.

The early New England yards produced a variety of light sailing vessels for short trips. Most of the ships were broad-beamed *sloops*, single-masted, not very long, and fairly wide across the middle. They were used for trading, fishing, ferrying, and transporting lumber and firewood. They became familiar sights along the New England coast and the riverways. Some of them made frequent trips to New Amsterdam, now New York City.

In 1641, the Massachusetts colony passed a law calling for inspection of all work on ships of over thirty tons, and for the correction of any work done badly. "The building of ships is a business of great importance for the common good, and therefore suitable care ought to be taken that it be well performed," part of the law stated.

By 1641, the building of small ships had become a major New England industry. In that year, a shipyard in Salem built the first American deepwater merchantman — a cargo vessel of three hundred tons, a large ship for its time. A

year later, a Boston shipyard finished the *Welcome,* another three-hundred-ton oceangoing cargo vessel. The slightly smaller two-hundred-ton oceangoing *Trial* was completed in Boston at about the same time. The *Trial* was an unusually well-built ship. She had a sailing life of at least fifteen years. Most American vessels of that period rarely lasted longer than ten years.

One of the largest ships of all was the four-hundred-ton *Seaforth.* She was built in Boston in 1645. Shipyards in Salem, Dorchester, Hingham, Scituate, Plymouth, and other Massachusetts seaside communities; in Warwick and Newport, Rhode Island; in New York; in Pennsylvania; and in New Hampshire and Connecticut coastal towns were all producing ships of various sizes. For the most part, these were ships of commerce. By this time, colonial ships were carrying on trade with the West Indies, Europe, and other parts of the world.

In 1682, William Penn started a shipbuilding business on the Delaware River. It soon became prosperous. The southern colonies also built some small vessels. But New England remained the most active shipbuilding region.

In 1690, one private shipyard in Portsmouth, New Hampshire, contracted with the British Admiralty to build a man-of-war. Never before had a British naval vessel been built outside the British Isles — or in a private shipyard, for that matter. In the home islands, British naval ships had always been built in government yards. Now the Admiralty reasoned that since the vessel's chief purpose would be to cruise the waters of New England, she could be built and maintained there more easily and cheaply. Moreover, Britain would not have to draw on her own limited reserves of timber for building the ship, but could use native American woods.

The Admiralty supplied the Portsmouth shipbuilder with the plan of the ship, or the *contract design*. A number of British shipwrights experienced in building naval ships were sent to the Portsmouth yard. Within a year, the *Falkland*, as she was called, made her first patrol in American waters. She was the first British naval vessel to be built in the colonies. In time, there would be more such Royal Navy warships built in American shipyards.

Although the building of the *Falkland* in a

colonial shipyard was a historic change of policy for the Admiralty, it seemed to be of little importance at the time. It was important to the American colonists, however. For, in this year 1690, they had received their first British-trained naval shipwrights — the best in the world. Some of these shipwrights remained in America and passed on their skills to colonial workers.

By the middle 1720's, British shipbuilders began to complain that the Crown was favoring colonial American shipbuilders — that there was not enough work in Britain, and more than enough work in America. Large numbers of British shipwrights began heading for America.

For the most part, the London government ignored the workers' complaints. Shipping was England's lifeline. She was the most powerful maritime nation in the world and she meant to stay that way. Great Britain needed ships — and the more quickly and cheaply she could get them, the better. The American colonists enjoyed the same privileges as English shipbuilders. They could construct as many vessels as they pleased, provided the ships flew the British flag.

By 1750, almost every major American port had become a shipbuilding center.

After 1750, however, Great Britain began to cut down on the size and number of naval ships built in the colonies. British naval authorities had come to believe that native American woods were inferior to British-grown woods. Actually, the American woods were not as much inferior as they were green, or poorly seasoned. Green timbers warped easily and had to be replaced often. Not only did they affect the way a ship ran, but also the cost of maintaining her.

It was becoming necessary to take far too many colonial-built naval vessels out of service for reconditioning and repair. The British authorities decided to allow the use of American woods for merchant ships and small, unimportant naval vessels only. They reserved the stout, better-seasoned English oak for first-class warships. By the time the American Revolution began in 1775, at least one-third of Britain's merchant fleet was being built in colonial American shipyards — chiefly in New England.

With the outbreak of war, the American colonies found themselves without a regular navy and facing the greatest maritime nation in the world. They did have a sizable fleet of merchant ships. Some two thousand of these were taken over by the Marine Committee of the Continental Congress and were armed and sent to sea as privately owned warships, or *privateers*.

These American-built ships and their crews were no match for the Royal Navy. But the speed and the ease with which the vessels could be handled enabled the Americans to destroy or capture about five hundred British vessels during the course of the Revolution. Most of these British ships were merchant vessels trying to deliver supplies to the British army in America. The loss of supplies was a severe blow to England's military plans in the colonies. It contributed eventually to her defeat.

As the Revolution went on, the Continental Congress tried to establish a regular navy. It ordered thirteen frigates to be built. Only eight were finished and sent to sea, where they were either destroyed or captured. Two of those captured — *Hancock* and *Providence* — were so well built that the Royal Navy added them to its own fleet of fighting ships.

The American Revolution was largely a land war, supported in its final months by a French fleet. Yet the American-built naval vessels, however few, were among the most reliable and seaworthy ships afloat. After the Revolution, unfortunately, the new United States government could not afford a navy. The ships were disarmed and sold as merchant vessels. America would be without a regular navy until the end of the eighteenth century, when it became necessary to protect American merchant ships from the Barbary Coast pirates in the Mediterranean Sea.

The end of the Revolution in 1781 not only brought independence to America; it also brought a renewed interest in commercial shipbuilding. Now no longer a group of colonies, the new United States was at liberty to trade wherever she pleased. Trade meant shipping. Shipping meant merchant ships. The American shipbuilders began to build a great merchant fleet that soon sailed the world over.

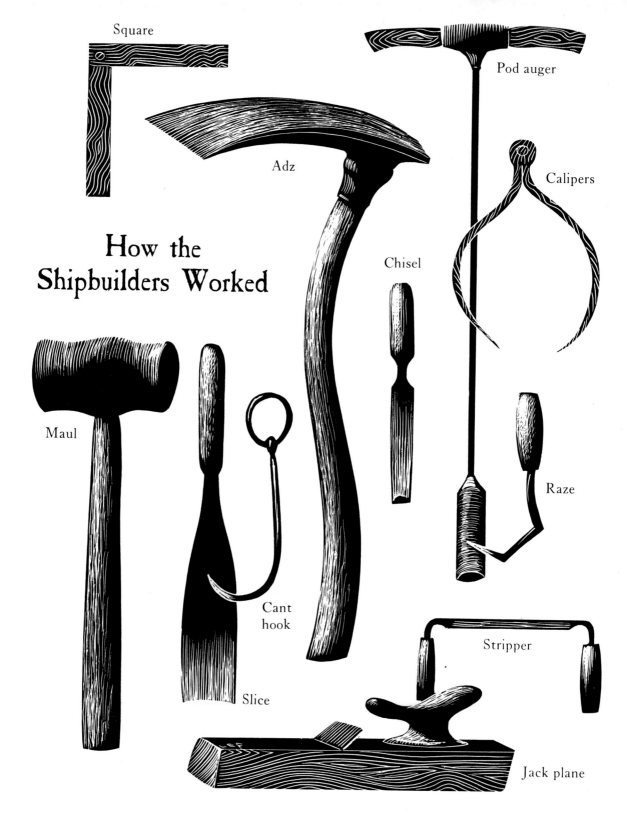

Square

Pod auger

Adz

Calipers

Chisel

How the
Shipbuilders Worked

Maul

Cant
hook

Raze

Stripper

Slice

Jack plane

The building of a wooden sailing ship during colonial times was complicated work. The construction of such a vessel was slow and painstaking, and usually took at least a year. The entire job was done by hand from start to finish. Every timber, plank, mast, spar, nut, bolt, rope, sail — and more — was handmade and hand fitted. As many as twenty to thirty different kinds of craftsmen — carpenters, cabinetmakers, ropemakers, caulkers, coopers, sailmakers, and the like — had a hand in the building of the ship.

In the finished vessel there were thousands of different parts, large and small. They had to operate efficiently while the ship was in motion. And they had to be joined so skillfully that the ship would not sail awkwardly at a crazy tilt, or list — or worse still, capsize and sink altogether.

A well-built vessel had to ride properly balanced in the water. She had to be well shaped and firmly put together. She had to be correctly rigged so as to resist the powerful forces of the sea while the winds moved her across the watery distances. And she had to be as watertight as possible. Too much water in her holds could not only spoil the cargo and rot the ship's timbers, but also could send her straight to the bottom of the sea.

In Britain, the naval vessels had been the most carefully planned. Shortly after the great British victory over the Spanish Armada in 1588, English naval architects, or ship designers, began to draw mathematical plans, or *drafts*, for whatever warship they had in mind. In many instances, scale models, accurate in every detail, were made from these drawings. The models demonstrated to members of the British Admiralty exactly what kind of ship was to be added to England's growing fleet.

British ship designers — and there were not many — paid little attention to merchant ships. Usually the design of a merchantman was left up to the owner of the proposed vessel, or to the shipbuilder, or even to the captain who would later command her.

The shipbuilding colonists in America used their skills chiefly to build a variety of commercial vessels. American shipbuilders tried to build ships that would do whatever job they were intended for and would weather whatever storm they met — ships whose appearance, handling, and hardiness would make their captains proud to sail aboard them. The shipbuilders were not always successful, but they aimed at producing good vessels.

The method of building wooden ships in colonial America varied according to the size, type, and location of the shipyard. Large yards like those in Boston and Philadelphia had excellent shipwrights and craftsmen of every description. Smaller shipyards in the outlying districts with few people were not as fortunate. Here, skilled shipbuilding labor was scarce. A craftsman might work on a ship one day and build a barn the next day. And if he was working on a ship, he would probably act as several craftsmen rolled into one: sawyer, joiner, caulker, and sailmaker.

In the large, important yards the ships were usually built on tracks, or *ways*. These were squared-off pieces of wood placed close together and leading into the water. The ships were sent down the ways into the water at some point in their building and were finished while afloat. Very rarely, small vessels were built in the neighboring forest, then during winter, when the snow was deep, were hitched to a team of horses or oxen and were dragged overland to the water.

Regardless of such differences, the work of building a wooden sailing ship in colonial America either began with a draft, or drawing; or with a scale model; or in a mold loft, a pattern shed. Or sometimes, ships were built "by eye" — with no plan at all.

The mold loft was a building with a large inside space. Here essential parts of a ship — usually its curved parts — were *lofted,* or drawn to their exact size and shape on a smooth floor. *Saw gangs* — men with saws — were then sent into the forests to find the oaks and other suitable woods whose shapes were closest to the markings on the floor of the mold loft. These trees were felled and hauled to the building site. Here the shipwrights in the loft measured the special dimensions and shapes needed, made simple wooden patterns of them, and handed the patterns over to the *sawyer,* the man who sawed up the wood. The sawyer would cut and fashion parts of the raw tree into the particular shapes given him.

The foundation of any ship — the chief sup-

port of its frame, or *ribs* — is the keel. It runs like a backbone from back to front along the center of the bottom of the boat. The keel is the very first part to be fashioned and put into place. Usually two, three, or four huge, squared-off timbers — depending on the length of the vessel — were bolted together after having been scarfed. To scarf two pieces of wood, the sawyer sliced their ends at an angle, then shaped and notched them to fit tightly together as they overlapped. Scarfing was the only way to join thick, straight pieces of wood to form curves. By varying the angles of the timber's sliced ends and joining these overlapping pieces, a workman could make any curve needed, or a straight section.

Once the keel was put together, it was lifted and placed on wooden blocks. Next, the sawyer cut a number of solid, angular pieces from a tree. Usually he tried to find the joint between a large branch and the trunk. These angular pieces, or *floors*, were squared off and bolted at intervals to the top of the keel.

More large pieces of wood were then scarfed into a graceful curve. (If the wood could be cut in one piece from a curving tree trunk, it would

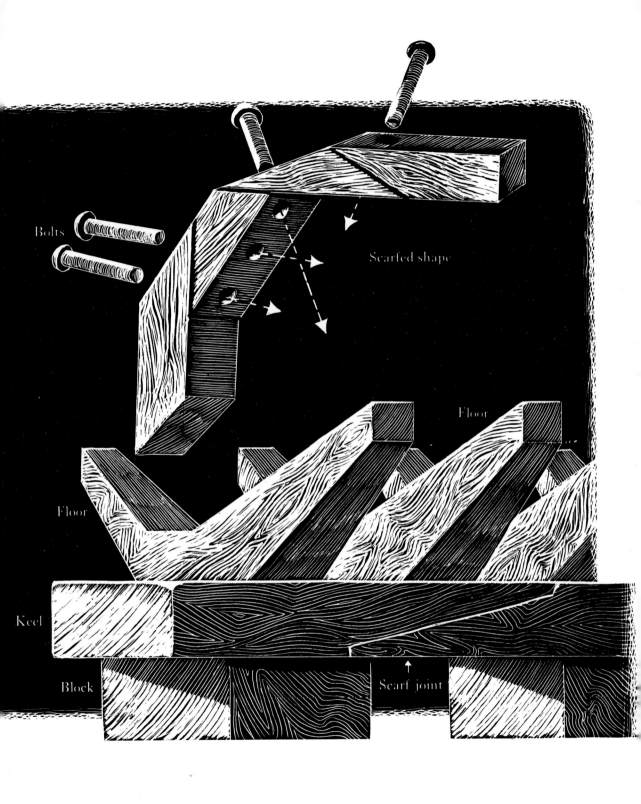

Bolts

Scarfed shape

Floor

Floor

Keel

Block

Scarf joint

prove to be stronger.) This curved section was fitted to one end of the keel and became the *stem*, the vertical center of the forward part, or *bow*, of the ship. A large, solid, straight piece of wood was then fitted to the other end of the keel to form the *sternpost*, the vertical center of the back end, or *stern*, of the ship.

The floors, which had already been carefully placed and bolted to the keel, were now ready to receive the *keelson*. The keelson, like the keel, was a scarfed beam. Its chief purpose was to strengthen the entire structure of the ship. It was laid on top of the floors — in the floor angle — and ran parallel to the keel. The keelson was fastened to the stem and sternpost and was bolted directly to the keel through the floors.

Next, the side curves of the ship's frame — her ribs — were made by scarfing straight and curved timbers. The curve of each rib was precisely formed. It varied according to the shape and curve of the ship's *hull* — the body of the ship. When the ribs were completed, they were fastened to the floor ends on both sides of the keel.

The inside of the ship was then given a cover of boards called a *ceiling*. The outside of the ship

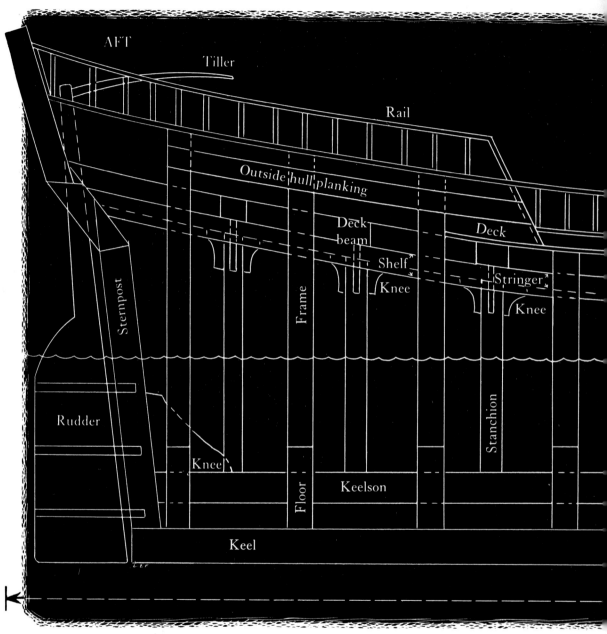

AFT

Tiller

Rail

Outside hull planking

Deck beam

Deck

Shelf

Stringer

Knee

Knee

Frame

Sternpost

Stanchion

Rudder

Knee

Floor

Keelson

Keel

Cross section of hull, eighteenth-century
single-masted ship.

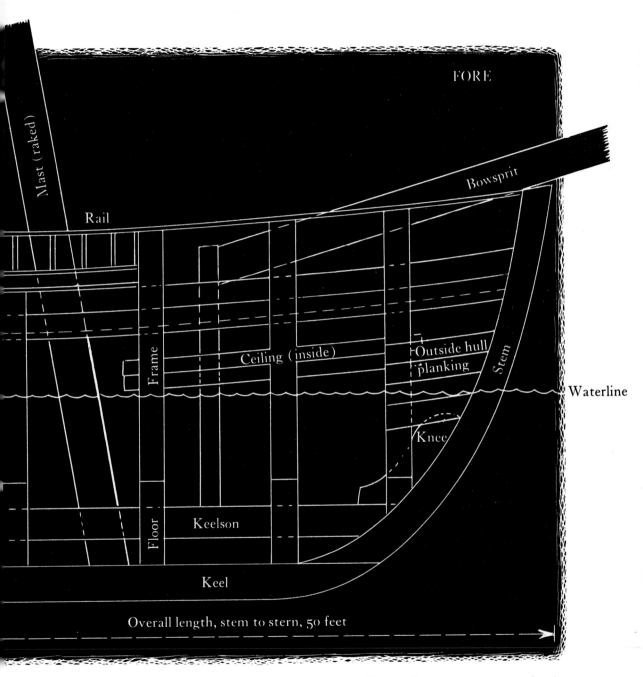

FORE

Mast (raked)

Rail

Bowsprit

Frame

Ceiling (inside)

Outside hull planking

Stem

Waterline

Knee

Floor

Keelson

Keel

Overall length, stem to stern, 50 feet

(For further details, see illustrations on pages 31 and 35)

was sheathed with planks. They covered the entire frame. The planks were usually of oak. Because they were stiff and straight, they had to be steamed until they were flexible. They were placed in *steam boxes*. When they were damp and hot and pliable, they were removed and carried to their position on the frame. There they were bent, then fastened to the frame with wooden pegs called *trunnels* or *treenails*. The trunnels were driven into holes previously bored through the frame and the ceiling. Each trunnel was then split on the inside of the ceiling so that a wooden wedge could be driven back into it, so tightening it.

Once the planks and ceiling were in place, other parts were added to the inside of the frame. Most important were the *shelves*. Fastened to the frame, the shelves held the *deck beams*. These beams crossed the width of the ship, and the deck planking was fastened to them. The deck beams were strengthened at the ends by wooden angles, or *knees*, which were bolted to the beams and to the frame. From the keelson, upright supports called *stanchions* ended in a beam called a *stringer*. This ran the length of the ship. The

stanchions and the stringer held up the middle part of the deck beams.

To prevent the sheathed frame, or hull, of the ship from tipping on the ways, a series of poles was wedged between its underside and the ground.

No matter how tightly the planks of the hull fitted together, there were still spaces between them. While the builders worked on the inside of the boat, *caulkers* stuffed these narrow spaces, or *seams*, with oakum. Oakum is a ropy fiber that has been soaked in a mild tar solution. The oakum was forced and pounded into every seam in the boat, to keep it from leaking. Not only were the seams in the hull filled with oakum, but so also was the tiny space around every treenail driven into the planking. Afterward, boiling pitch was applied to the oakum caulking, which was scraped smooth after it had hardened. Now the ship was reasonably watertight. A good soaking in the sea itself would swell the hull planking and make the vessel even less likely to leak.

When the caulking was completed, work on the vessel was either finished where she stood, or she

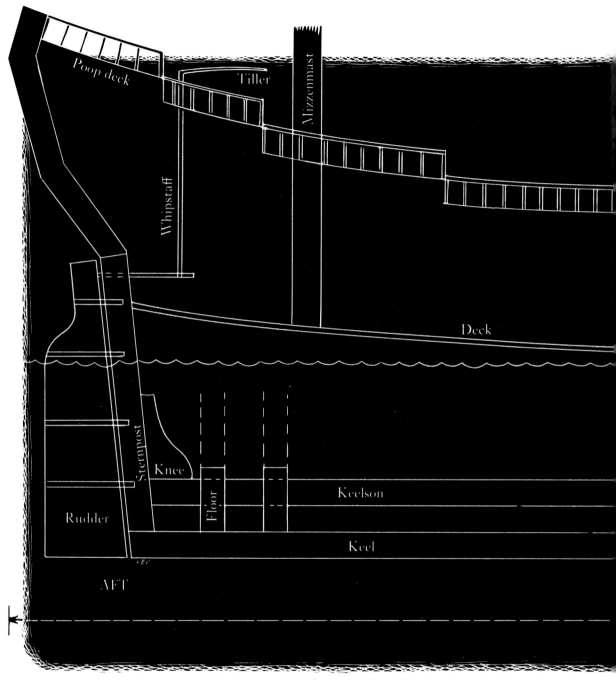

Cross section of hull, seventeenth-century
three-masted vessel, showing levels for
securing masts.

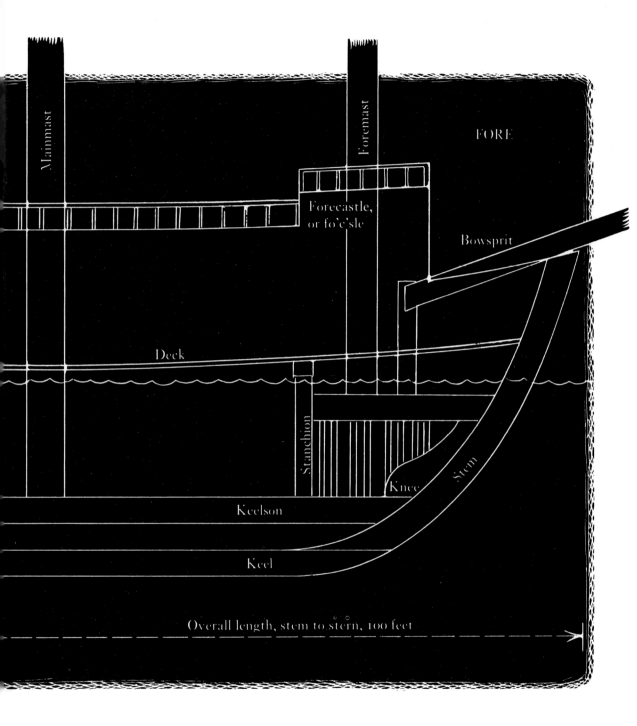

Mainmast

Foremast

FORE

Forecastle, or fo'c'sle

Bowsprit

Deck

Stanchion

Knee

Stem

Keelson

Keel

Overall length, stem to stern, 100 feet

was launched and completed while floating and tied to a wharf.

If the ship was to be launched, a *cradle*, a wooden framework, was built to support her as she slid down the ways. The ways themselves were well greased to ensure a smooth launching. Workmen were positioned at every wedge or pole supporting the ship's underside. At a given signal, each man struck the bottom of his wedge, driving it slightly inward and straighter. This lifted the entire ship just enough so that workmen could pull away the blocks upon which she rested. Then the wedges were all removed except for one at the stern. When this wedge was knocked out, the ship slid into the water, stern first. She was supported by the cradle. After bobbing about for a bit, the vessel was towed to the wharf and work on her was continued.

Sailing ships of the colonial period usually had one, two, or three masts to carry the sails. Most of the ships also had a spar that rose out of the ship and thrust forward from the stem. This was called the *bowsprit*.

Once the ship was launched, there was the question of masts. How many should there be?

otted lines indicate posi-
n of vessel and wedges
fore wedges are struck
ward and vessel is lifted
 that support blocks
n be removed.

Support

blocks

Support stakes
or wedges

How should they be fastened to the frame, and at what angle? In most instances, the answer depended on the kind of ship, her size, and the job she was intended to do. These things would also determine what kind of rigging — ropes, chains, or other lines — would operate the sails and support the masts and help keep them in place.

Some masts were *raked*, or slanted at steep angles. Others stood straight up. More than likely, the *mainmast*, or center mast — the tallest and thickest of all the spars — rose from the keelson, to which it was fastened. Its supporting *stays*, or lines, were secured to the hull. If an uncommonly tall mast was needed, it was made in sections and joined together by *fastening caps*. Other masts like the *mizzenmast*, or rear mast, and the *foremast*, or front mast, might be fastened at different levels in the ship's interior. These spars, too, might be made in sections if the design required it.

The sails were made in buildings called *sail lofts*. Like all other parts of the ship, sails were made by hand. They were woven out of heavy flax, cut to the proper shapes, and hand sewn.

Ropes of all sizes were used aboard seven-

Earing

Yard loop

Mast

Lift lines

Yard

Head

Leech

Leech

Foot

Clew

Clew

Square sail,
raised on mast

Grommet

Tabling

Clew (corner)

Boltrope

Punch

Knife

Awl

Section of rope walk, showing previously spun
cords in the beginning stages of being
"whirled," or twisted.

teenth- and eighteenth-century sailing ships.
Without the thousands of yards of strong rope,
there would have been no way to control the
movement of the ship. Rope was made by the
ropemaker in a long, enclosed space called a *rope
walk*. Here, strands of hemp were endlessly
twisted by hand into particular thicknesses and
lengths.

Blocks for hoisting; *ratlines* for rope ladders; a
rudder and wheel, or tiller connected by a *whip
staff* for steering were only a few more of the
hundreds of essential parts of a sailing ship.

Sometimes large and expensive ships had a skin
of copper sheeting nailed to the underside of their
hulls. This metal skin helped to prevent the quick
rotting of timbers below the waterline. From
time to time, colonial American ships were
painted. If the entire ship was not painted, at
least some part of it, such as its decorative wood-
work, might be. The color depended mostly on
what paint happened to be available. It mattered
little in the end, because most of the paint flaked,
peeled, and disappeared after a few weeks at sea.

Rail

Three-strand rope

Post

Five-strand rope

Cords

Table wheel

Whirl wheel

Moreover, paint was expensive and difficult to obtain in large quantities. Many a colonial American ship went to sea unpainted.

Shipbuilding in the American colonies was a combination of necessity and imagination. Colonial America, on the seaboard, was constantly challenged by the mystery and lure of the sea. Ships were the only link to the world that most American colonists had left behind — England and the European continent. Ships made wider trade possible. That trade brought European civilization to the American wilderness. Ships brought people to America. They helped America grow with stunning speed.

Index